Shelflisting Music

Guidelines for Use with the Library of Congress Classification: M

Second Edition

Richard P. Smiraglia

*Music Library Association
Technical Reports, No. 30*

The Scarecrow Press, Inc.
Lanham, Maryland • Toronto • Plymouth, UK
and
Music Library Association, Inc.
2008

SCARECROW PRESS, INC.

Published in the United States of America
by Scarecrow Press, Inc.
A wholly owned subsidiary of
The Rowman & Littlefield Publishing Group, Inc.
4501 Forbes Boulevard, Suite 200, Lanham, Maryland 20706
www.scarecrowpress.com

Estover Road
Plymouth PL6 7PY
United Kingdom

Copyright © 2008 by Richard P. Smiraglia

All rights reserved. No part of this publication may be reproduced, stored in a retrieval system, or transmitted in any form or by any means, electronic, mechanical, photocopying, recording, or otherwise, without the prior permission of the publisher.

British Library Cataloguing in Publication Information Available

Library of Congress Cataloging-in-Publication Data

Smiraglia, Richard P., 1952–
  Shelflisting music : guidelines for use with the Library of Congress classification, M / by Richard P. Smiraglia. — 2nd ed.
    p. cm. — (Music Library Association technical reports ; no. 30)
  Includes bibliographical references (p.).
  ISBN-13: 978-0-8108-5418-5 (pbk. : alk. paper)
  ISBN-10: 0-8108-5418-X (pbk. : alk. paper)
  1. Shelflisting. 2. Classification—Music. 3. Classification, Library of Congress. I. Title.

ML111.S64 2007
025.4'28—dc22   2007028615

☉™ The paper used in this publication meets the minimum requirements of American National Standard for Information Sciences—Permanence of Paper for Printed Library Materials, ANSI/NISO Z39.48-1992.
Manufactured in the United States of America.

Music Library Association Technical Reports Series

Edited by H. Stephen Wright

1. *SLACC: The Partial Use of the Shelf List as a Classed Catalog by the Music Library Association Cataloging and Classification Committee*, 1973.
2. *Directory of Music Library Automation Projects* compiled by Garett Bowles, 1973; 2nd ed., 1979.
3. *Proceedings of the Institute on Library of Congress Music Cataloging Policies and Procedures* edited by David Sommerfield, 1975.
4. *The Classification and Cataloging of Sound Recordings: An Annotated Bibliography* by Barbara Knisely Gaeddert, 1977, 2nd ed., 1981.
5. *Recordings of Non-Western Music, Subject and Added Entry Access* by Judith Kaufman, 1977.
6. *Index to Audio Equipment Reviews, 1978* by Arne Jon Arneson and Stuart Milligan, 1979.
7. *Shelving Capacity in the Music Library* by Robert Michael Fling, 1981.
8. *Index to Audio Equipment Reviews, 1979* by Arne Jon Arneson and Stuart Milligan, 1980.
9. *Shelflisting Music: Guidelines for Use with the Library of Congress Classification: M* by Richard P. Smiraglia, 1981.
10. *Index to Audio Equipment Reviews, 1980* by Arne Jon Arneson and Stuart Milligan, 1981.
11. *The Acquisition and Cataloging of Music and Sound Recordings: A Glossary* by Suzanne Thorin, 1984.
12. *Index to Audio Equipment Reviews, 1981* by Arne Jon Arneson and Stuart Milligan, 1982.
13. *The MARC Music Format: From Inception to Publication* by Donald Seibert, 1982.
14. *Library of Congress Subject Headings for Recordings of Western Non-Classical Music* by Judith Kaufman, 1983.
15. *Sheet Music Cataloging and Processing: A Manual Prepared for the Brown University Library Title II-C Sheet Music Cataloging Project* by Sarah J. Shaw and Lauralee Shiere, 1984.
16. *Authority Control in Music Libraries: Proceedings of the Music Library Association Preconference, March 5, 1985* edited by Ruth Tucker, 1989.
17. *Planning and Caring for Library Audio Facilities* edited by James P. Cassaro, 1989.

18. *Careers in Music Librarianship: Perspectives From the Field* compiled by Carol Tatian, 1991.
19. *In Celebration of Revised 780: Music in the Dewey Decimal Classification, Edition 20* compiled by Richard B. Wursten, 1990.
20. *Space Utilization in Music Libraries* compiled by James P. Cassaro, 1992.
21. *Archival Information Processing for Sound Recordings: The Design of a Database for the Rodgers and Hammerstein Archives of Recorded Sound* by David Thomas, 1992.
22. *Collection Assessment in Music Libraries* edited by Jane Gottlieb, 1994.
23. *Knowing the Score: Preserving Collections of Music* compiled by Mark Roosa and Jane Gottlieb, 1994.
24. *World Music in Music Libraries* edited by Carl Rahkonen, 1994.
25. *Cataloging Musical Moving Image Material: A Guide to the Bibliographic Control of Videorecordings and Films of Musical Performances and Other Music-Related Moving Image Material: With Examples in MARC Format* edited by Lowell Ashley, 1996.
26. *Guide to Writing Collection Development Policies for Music*, by Amanda Maple and Jean Morrow, 2001.
27. *Music Librarianship at the Turn of the Century*, edited by Richard Griscom, assistant editor Amanda Maple, 2000.
28. *Cataloging Sheet Music: Guidelines for Use with AACR2 and the MARC format*, compiled and edited by Lois Schultz and Sarah Shaw, 2003.
29. *Careers in Music Librarianship: Traditions and Transitions*, edited by Paula Elliot, associate editor Linda Blair, 2004.
30. *Shelflisting Music: Guidelines for Use with the Library of Congress Classification: M*, Second edition, by Richard P. Smiraglia, 2008.

Contents

Foreword to the Second Edition	vii
Introduction	ix
The Shelflisting Process: A Flowchart Analysis	1
Work Number Tables	9
Distinguishing Elements and Translations	11
Guidelines for Shelflisting Music Materials	13
Glossary	23
The Library of Congress Music Shelflist	27
Flowcharts	29
About the Author	37

Foreword to the Second Edition

I hardly remember the origins of this pamphlet. I think (but this might turn out to be apocryphal) that I first constructed it as a guide for use by catalogers in my department at the University of Illinois Music Library. But then again, that just seems like a logical explanation. Equally logical would be that I wrote it as a guide for my own use, because in those days I was forever trying to systematize what seemed very complex practices. In those days we had a real card shelflist, and at Illinois as many other music libraries it was kept in a public area so it could serve double duty as a classified catalog.

Rumor has it (that would be e-mail from R. Griscom) that Richard Griscom at some point used the flowcharts to create a computer program that could assign call numbers. If so, it suggests I got something right about the sequence of operations. In any event, *Shelflisting Music* was my first publication, and I am gratified that it has been so well-received that the publishers have asked me to generate a new edition.

I suppose that term is a bit of a misnomer as well—this "second edition" is little changed from the first. Bibliographers will see that the documents are very different from each other. But reviewers will note little of consequence differs between the two. I have removed every infelicity of English grammar I could. Given the complexity of the operations described there are some very convoluted sentences here and there. I was unable to simplify them in any useful way, and for that I apologize. Other than that, I have updated all of the references throughout and checked to see that this remains in conformity with Library of Congress practice. As before, wherever the reader encounters an *optional* instruction, that is a departure from LC practice that I recommended based on my own experience as a cataloger of music at Illinois.

Introduction

Shelflisting of music materials in the *Library of Congress Classification (LCC)* can be a complex process. Because of the variety of ways in which music is composed and published, the relatively logical means of title-associated book numbers (also known as "cuttering"), which is used for most book materials, is often of little use. Much of the instrumental repertory carries generic titles (e.g., Sonata, Symphony, Quartet, etc.) that could render a prolific composer's output in any particular category quite muddled should shelf arrangement by title be attempted. Opus or thematic index numbers, which can be extremely useful for shelf arrangement, are not always readily apparent. Because the librarian may find it desirable to sort scores of dramatic works according to the languages into which their texts have been translated, opus numbers might not be useful even if they are available. These factors, among others, must all be considered by the person shelflisting music materials in order to achieve an optimum shelf arrangement that will best benefit the collection's users.

The shelflisting process in music is heavily dependent on the completed bibliographic description. The uniform title in particular supplies many useful elements (original title(s), thematic index, opus or serial enumeration, key, date of composition, language of translation of sung or spoken text). These same elements, which are used to bring logical order to bibliographic descriptions in traditional catalogs, serve also as effective tools to provide the most useful arrangement on the shelf.

The guidelines presented here represent an updating and expansion of those first set in print by Virginia Cunningham in 1961,[1] and incorporate rules presented by Helvi Jaakola at the 1971 Institute on Library of Congress Music Cataloging Policies and Procedures.[2] These pages reflect shelflisting practice at the Library of Congress as determined from the aforementioned sources, LC printed cards for music and various other LC publications. Additional suggestions drawn from experience have been incorporated. In all cases these suggestions are clearly

x   Introduction

labeled as optional. Since works classified in ML (Literature of music) and MT (Music instruction and study) are shelflisted in a manner similar to that used for other material, these instructions are primarily for use with works placed in class M.

In addition, a flowchart analysis accompanies a detailed discussion of the decision-making process by which call numbers are constructed for materials in class M as a means of providing guidance for those not familiar with the classification of music materials. A glossary of technical terms used in this report appears as the final section.

Notes

1. Virginia Cunningham, "Shelflisting Music," *Music Library Association Notes: Supplement for Members* 31 (Feb. 1961), pp. 11-13.

2. Helvi Jaakola, "Shelflisting of Music Materials," in *Proceedings of the Institute on Library of Congress Music Cataloging Policies and Procedures, January 26-27, 1971, Coolidge Auditorium, Library of Congress, Washington, D.C.*, ed. David Sommerfield (Ann Arbor, MI: Music Library Association, 1975), pp. 73-80.

The Shelflisting Process: A Flowchart Analysis

Flowcharting, "the schematic representation of a sequence of operations,"[1] has proven useful in recent years for analysis and instruction of many library operations. Because of the complexity of the shelflisting process in class M (a single call number can require as many as forty-six separate decisions and operations) the shelflister must remain aware of a variety of options that might appear to be suitable in any given situation, choosing those options that will provide the most convenient shelf arrangement for browsing or retrieval in any particular class. The chart presented here (*see* Figure 1) offers a logical sequence of questions or decisions (represented by diamond-shaped boxes) the answers to which indicate the subsequent direction of the activity (indicated by arrows).

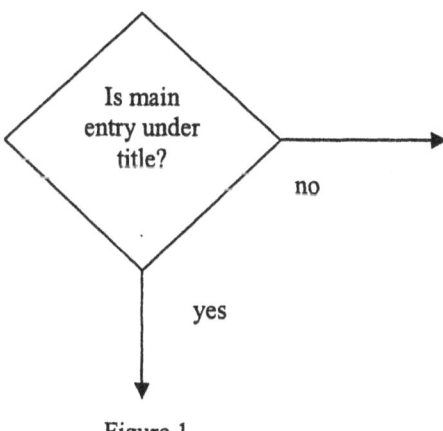

Figure 1

Operations are indicated by rectangular boxes (*see* Figure 2).

```
┌─────────────────┐
│  Assign date of │
│  publication    │
└─────────────────┘
```

Figure 2

Excerpts from the master chart accompany this discussion as a means of illustrating specific groups of operations. These excerpts are identified as Flowcharts 1-2 (p. 29-30), and they are linked in sequence with pentagonal boxes bearing Greek letters (*see* Figure 3).

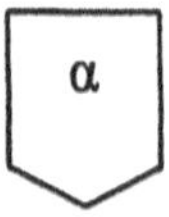

Figure 3

The various operations are described in detail in the second section of this report, "Guidelines for Shelflisting Music Materials." It is suggested that the reader first become familiar with the sequence of operations described below before grappling with the guidelines.

Some steps that are designated as optional in the guidelines have been included in the chart in order to demonstrate the sequence of decisions that would be required to utilize them. Once familiar with the range of options available, the experienced shelflister will be able to delete entire segments as deemed necessary.

In constructing a call number, the first step after classification involves a sub-routine, which is demonstrated by an auxiliary chart (*see* Flowchart 4A, p. 35). This chart defines the method by which natural language (i.e., names or words in a title) is converted to alphanumeric symbols, usually referred to as "cutters" or work numbers. This is a procedure that might be repeated several times in the course of call number construction.

The first step is to determine the letters that need to be symbolized (usually the composer's or editor's surname or the first significant word of the title) and then refer to the appropriate table(s) to determine the numerical symbols that represent those letters. For example, to establish a symbol to represent the name Mozart one would first consult Table 4 (p. 9) since the initial letter M falls into the category of "other initial consonants." For the second letter "o" the table indicates a numerical symbol "6." Since this is a main entry, which will probably require a second digit, the third letter "z" is checked in Table 5 (p. 10) where the symbol "9" is indicated. The numeric symbols are then appended to the initial letter in sequence to construct the work number, "M69." Some selected examples are:

Evans	.E92
Schubert	.S38
Quantz	.Q36

Additional examples appear throughout the guidelines.[2]

The length of the symbol is dependent on its function in the call number. While specific suggestions are included in the guidelines, the shelflister should remember that the Library of Congress attempts to keep author notation as short and simple as possible. Furthermore, the Library of Congress makes no attempt to assign fixed cutters to specific composers. As a result the symbol for a particular name is constant only within a single class.[3] The shelflister should bear in mind that room must be left in the shelflist to accommodate future acquisitions, and that each entry in a particular class must be added in such a way so as to preserve alphabetic order.[4]

Adjustments might be required in order to establish an appropriate alphabetical sequence within each class. This will be apparent when the shelflist is consulted at the end of the call number process. If, for instance, a work by Igor Stravinsky appears in the shelflist with the work number .S77, a conflict will arise should a work by Soulima Stravinsky be entered in the same class. The shelflister might elect to enter the later work under .S78, and this would indeed preserve the alphabetical sequence. But remembering that work numbers are decimal numbers and are therefore infinitely expandable, a better option might be to cutter for the fourth letter "a" thus placing the work in .S772. This choice would leave space in the sequence for later addition of works by persons whose names begin Stu . . . to be placed in .S78, as well as for works by composers whose names begin Stre . . . which could be placed in .S774. This technique is especially valuable in classes such as M25, M11, and M1045, which are catchall classes for piano, organ and orchestral music respectively.

The procedure outlined above for construction of author numbers is also used to construct title work numbers (explained below). For this reason the reader can be directed to "assign work number (Flowchart

4A)" at four distinct points during the shelflisting process, which are represented by hexagonal boxes (*see* Figure 4).

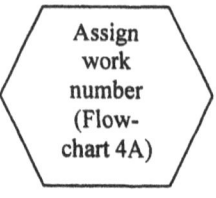

Figure 4

Upon reaching the connector labeled "RETURN" at the end of Flowchart 4A, the reader should in every instance return to the place in the flowchart where the direction to Flowchart 4A occurred and proceed from that point. This procedure should also be employed in assigning work numbers for instrument, text, etc. as specified in the classification tables. In most instances, Library of Congress's own numbers are specified in the tables (e.g., M2079, etc.).

As reflected in the main chart, there are four broad areas in the construction of a call number:

    1) assignment of an initial work number to represent the main entry (discussed above);

    2) addition of a second element, which is either one of four specific distinguishing elements (*see* Table 6, p. 11); or

    3) a second work number (also referred to as a double cutter) to represent the title of the work; and

    4) distinguishing variant editions of the same work.

The next step depends upon whether the symbol just assigned represents a title main entry, or main entry under composer (compiler, editor, etc.). If it is under title the process is now virtually complete and the reader is directed to the steps for distinguishing editions (about which more later) and a final shelflist check. If, however, the work number represents a composer, the next several steps will be used to establish the second element of the call number (*see* Flowchart 1).

Development of this area of the call number is roughly similar to the construction of a generic uniform title. Several distinguishing elements (Table 6, no. 1-4), which may be present in the uniform title, or readily available in standard reference sources, can be used to provide a convenient shelf arrangement of a composer's work in any given class.

(Note that these four elements are listed in order of preference; normally only one is used in any particular call number.) The most convenient is the opus or thematic index number. In some cases the thematic index number may be preferable to the opus number when both exist. (For more detailed information, see section C1.1 in the guidelines, p. 14.) If available, it can be added as the element immediately following the composer's work number, and the shelflister may proceed directly to the steps used to distinguish arrangements or editions.

If there is no opus or thematic index number, the next preferred element is a serial number if the class is one in which the name of the class equates with the titles of a work (i.e., Piano sonatas, M23). One may also wish to deviate from the chart at this point if it becomes apparent that all of a composer's works in a particular class have serial numbers but only some have opus numbers. A decision to prefer the serial numbers in this instance will provide a convenient chronological shelf arrangement of that composer's works. Alternately, the works may be assigned whatever elements are available in the order of preference illustrated in Table 6 and the works may be interfiled according to that sequence.

If thematic index, opus, or serial numbers are not present, the key in which the piece was composed (or tonal center for later works) may be added as the second element if it is present in the uniform title. The final distinguishing element (almost always used only as a last resort) is the date of composition of the work. This too must be present in the uniform title if it is to be used in the call number. If this device is used it is wise to enclose it in parentheses (according to Library of Congress guidelines) to distinguish it from a date of publication, which may be used later to distinguish editions of the work.

When no distinguishing elements are available, the title becomes the source for the second element. If the title of the work equates with the name of the class and no distinguishing elements are available, the shelflister may choose to stop at this point. Otherwise a second work number is assigned to represent the title of the work. For this step, the auxiliary chart (*see* Flowchart 4A) must be consulted to determine the appropriate symbol.

For dramatic vocal works (operas, oratorios, etc.) the guidelines (section E) should be consulted. It may be wise to prefer a title work number (for example .F5 for Beethoven's *Fidelio* instead of op. 72) despite the presence of distinguishing numerical elements. Since these categories of works almost always have distinctive titles, this can provide a more convenient shelf arrangement for browsers expecting to find a composer's works arranged on the shelf alphabetically by title. It might also be desirable to add a digit to represent the language of the translation of the text as does the Library of Congress.

Once this element has been assigned, the chart directs the shelflister to a series of steps that will further refine the call number, including addition of extra digits to represent the title of an excerpt or the language of a translated text, as well as assignment of elements to represent the name of an arranger, editor or publisher where desirable.

The next question is whether or not the work in hand is an excerpt from a larger work (*see* Flowchart 2). If so, it must be determined whether the excerpt is numbered, or has a distinctive title of its own. If the excerpt is numbered (this information is ascertained from the uniform title assigned to the work), the number is added following either the distinguishing element or title cutter that represents the work as a whole. If the excerpt is titled, a digit (from Table 5) is added to the title work number to represent the first significant word of the title of the excerpt. When the excerpt symbol follows a distinguishing element, a new work number must be developed (*see* Flowchart 4A) to represent the title of the excerpt.

If the work under consideration is one whose text has been translated (this information will appear in the uniform title also) it might be desirable to add a digit to the title cutter to represent the language of the translation. This step will apply primarily to piano-vocal scores of dramatic works such as operas, oratorios and cantatas. If the text is printed in several languages, the extra digit should represent that language listed first in the uniform title. These digits are derived from Table 7 (p. 11).

When the work is an arrangement, a digit from Table 5 may be added to the title work number, or a second work number (from Flowchart 4A) added following a distinguishing element to represent the name of the arranger. If the work has been arranged by its original composer this element will represent that composer's name. As usual, discretion must be exercised by the shelflister. The Library of Congress employs this option only for resolution of conflicts for works that have appeared in many similar arrangements. While large research libraries might prefer always to distinguish arrangements in this fashion, thus providing alphabetical array automatically should a new version be acquired, smaller libraries might find it best to follow the more conservative approach of the Library of Congress.

It is sometimes desirable to distinguish various editions of a work in this manner (with the addition of an extra digit to the title work number), as well. The Library of Congress favors assigning the date of publication to represent each edition (*see* Flowchart 3, p. 31). However, another option, which is useful in large research collections, is to first distinguish each edition with an extra digit or second work number (representing editor or publisher in that order of preference) as discussed above for arrangements. Dates may then be added to distinguish issues of a particular edition.[5]

At this stage the potential call number is complete; the next step will be to consult the shelflist. Some adjustments might be required in the alphanumeric elements if the number is not unique or if it will place the item outside the desired alphabetical sequence. The procedure discussed earlier in reference to adjustment of initial work numbers should be employed now to resolve any conflicts.

The reader will note that collections have not been discussed, even though the flowchart illustrates a point at which they are to be sorted from works that are considered separate. This is because of the unique but simple way in which collections are shelflisted. If the work is a collection of pieces by several persons (usually three or more) the main entry will be under title and only a work number representing the title is required.

For collections of works by one composer the first consideration is the nature of the collection. If it is a series of similar works that bear sequential (or collective) thematic index or opus numbers, the numbers are assigned in the same manner in which thematic index or opus numbers are assigned to call numbers for separate publications. Other collections of works by one composer receive a second work number, which represents the name of the editor or publisher of the collection. Examples of each type appear in Section D of the guidelines (p. 17).

Notes

1. William Morris, ed., *The American Heritage Dictionary of the English Language* (Boston: American Heritage Pub. Co., 1969), p. 505.

2. Examples, and the most recent Library of Congress book number tables, from which these tables derive appear in Library of Congress. Cataloging Policy and Support Office. *Subject Cataloging Manual. Shelflisting*. 2nd ed. Washington, D.C.: Cataloging Distribution Service, Library of Congress, 1995.

3. It should be noted that the author numbers on Library of Congress printed cards reflect the holdings of the Library of Congress as represented in its shelflist and are therefore not necessarily very useful in providing guidance for the shelflister. Many classes reflect years of changing policy decisions; in approximately 300 classes and subclasses author numbers are not used by the Library of Congress for shelf arrangement. For a more detailed discussion see Jaakola, pp. 73-74.

4. *Cataloging Service Bulletin* 3, p. 20.

5. For a good discussion of the concept of musical edition see D. W. Krummel, comp., *Guide for Dating Early Published Music: A Manual of Bibliographical Practices* (Hackensack, N.J.: Joseph Boonin, 1974), pp. 30-48.

Work Number Tables

The following tables are from *Cataloging Service Bulletin* 3, p. 19-20.

TABLE 1: WORK NUMBERS AFTER INITIAL VOWELS

for the second letter:	b	d	l,m	n	p	r	s,t	u-y
use number:	2	3	4	5	6	7	8	9

TABLE 2: WORK NUMBERS AFTER INITIAL LETTER S

for the second letter:	a	ch	e	h,i	m-p	t	u
use number:	2	3	4	5	6	7-8	9

TABLE 3: WORK NUMBERS AFTER INITIAL LETTERS Q-UU

for the third letter:	a	e	i	o	r	y
use number:	3	4	5	6	7	9

for names beginning:	QA-QT
use:	2-29

TABLE 4: WORK NUMBERS AFTER OTHER INITIAL CONSONANTS

for the second letter:	a	e	i	o	r	u	y
use number:	3	4	5	6	7	8	9

TABLE 5: WORK NUMBERS WHEN AN ADDITIONAL DIGIT IS PREFERRED

for the third letter:	a-d	e-h	i-l	m	n-q	r-t	u-w	x-z
use number:	2*	3	4	5	6	7	8	9

*optional for third letter a or b

Distinguishing Elements and Translations

The following tables are from Jaakola, pp. 75, 78.

TABLE 6: DISTINGUISHING ELEMENTS IN ORDER OF PREFERENCE

1. Opus or thematic index number
2. Serial number
3. Key
4. Date of composition
5. Work number for title
6. No second element

TABLE 7: NUMBERS FOR LANGUAGES OF TRANSLATIONS

Language	Number
English	2
French	3
German	4
Italian & Latin	5
Russian	7
Spanish	8
Swedish	9

Guidelines for Shelflisting Music Materials

These guidelines represent Library of Congress policy. *Options* are the suggestions of this author. In the examples that follow, each element of the call number is placed on a separate line. In each instance the portion of the call number being illustrated as well as the elements of the entry being represented are underscored.

A: TITLE MAIN ENTRY

The work number is formulated according to Tables 1-5 using the first word of the title excluding initial articles. One letter and at least two digits are usually required for title main entry (though additional digits may be necessary depending on the library's holdings in any particular class). Ordinarily no further notation is required.

Example 1: M
1630.18
.*S95*

*Sum*mer in the country . . .

B: COMPOSER (i.e., NAME) MAIN ENTRY

The work number is formulated according to Tables 1-5 using the first element of the entry. One letter and one digit are required, though more digits may be necessary in some classes.

Example 2: M
23
.*M69*

*Mo*zart, Wolfgang Amadeus, 1756-1791.

C: DISTINGUISHING ELEMENTS
C1: OPUS OR THEMATIC INDEX NUMBER

If an opus or thematic index number is given, it is added as the next element after the work number.

Example 3: M   MacDowell, Edward, 1860-1908.
               23   [Sonatas, piano, no. 4, *op. 59*]
               .M33
               op. 59

C1.1: THEMATIC INDEX OR OPUS NUMBER CONFLICTS

The Library of Congress prefers thematic index numbers when opus numbering problems exist and a reputable thematic index is available. There are also instances when both are used so that only the unnumbered works of Beethoven, for example, are referred to by Kinsky numbers. In all such instances, the preference will be apparent from the uniform title assigned to the work.

Example 4: M   Beethoven, Ludwig van, 1770-1827.
               857   [Rondino, woodwinds, horns (2),
               .B44   *K. 25*, E major]
               K. 25   Rondino in E flat major . . . op.
                           posth. . . .

               M   Vivaldi, Antonio, 1678-1741.
               1140   [Concertos, oboes (2), clarinets (2),
               .V58   string orchestra, *RV 559*, C major]
               RV 559

Optionally, if an opus or thematic index number can be determined from standard reference sources, it may be added to the bibliographic description as a note and may then be used as the next element in the call number.

Example 5: M   Hovhaness, Alan, 1911-2000.
               1145   [Armenian rhapsody, no. 3]
               .H68   Armenian rhapsody : no. 3, string
               op. 189   orchestra ...
                           ["Op. 189."]

C2: OTHER DISTINGUISHING ELEMENTS

When an opus or thematic index number is lacking, other distinguishing elements may be used if available, in the following order of preference:

C2.1: SERIAL NUMBER

In those classes in which the uniform title equates with the name of the class (e.g., Piano sonatas = M23; Symphonies = M1001) serial numbers may be added as the next element.

Example 6: M   Hiller, Lejaren Arthur, 1924-1994.
23   [Sonatas, piano, *no. 4*]
.H54
no. 4

M   Bacewicz, Grażyna.
219   [Sonatas, violin, piano, *no. 3*]
.B33
no. 3

Optionally, when works by one composer in the same class do not all have opus numbers, prefer serial numbers if they have been established.

Example 7: M   Krenek, Ernst, 1900-1991.
23   [Sonatas, piano, *no. 2*, op. 59]
.K74
no. 2

M   Krenek, Ernst, 1900-1991.
23   [Sonatas, piano, *no. 4*]
.K74
no. 4

C2.2: KEY

The key in which the piece is composed may be used as the next element of the call number when it is used as a distinguishing element in the uniform title of the work.

Example 8: M   Ravel, Maurice, 1875-1937.
            1010   [Concertos, piano, orchestra, *G major*]
            .R38
            G maj.

C2.3: DATE OF COMPOSITION

The year in which the piece was composed may be added when it is used as a distinguishing element in the uniform title for the work; this should be placed in parentheses to distinguish it from dates used to identify editions.

Example 9: M   Bartók, Bela, 1881-1945.
            219   [Sonatas, violin, piano *(1903)*]
            .B37
            (1903)

C3: WORK NUMBER FOR TITLE (OR DOUBLE CUTTER)

For works lacking the aforementioned distinguishing elements, for works whose titles do not equate with the name of the class, and for all dramatic vocal works (see also Section E), a double cutter or second work number representing uniform title, or in its absence, the title proper is added as the second element. These symbols are derived from Tables 1-4 and ordinarily require only one letter and one digit.

Example 10: M   Komori, Akihiro.
            1520   *Dr*ums in the night ...
            .K66
            D7

            M   Cruft, Adrian.
            452   [*Su*ite, string quartet]
            .C78
            S8

[Note: "Suite" in a quartet class is considered a distinctive title.]

C4: TITLES THAT EQUATE WITH THE NAME OF THE CLASS

For works whose uniform titles equate with the name of the class, and are either the first entry of a composer in that class, or are works which can be determined to be the only work by a composer which will be entered in that class (usually determined only for composers no longer living), no further notation beyond the initial work number need be used.

Example 11: M   *Mak*ris, Andreas, 1930-2005.
               452   [Quartet, strings]
               .M34

[Note: So far no other string quartet by this composer is known; if a "no. 2" arrives, it can be added in the correct sequence.]

D: COLLECTIONS
D1: WORKS BY ONE COMPOSER WITH SEQUENTIAL OPUS OR THEMATIC INDEX NUMBERS

Collections of works in the same musical form by one composer that bear sequential or collective opus or thematic index numbers utilize those numbers in the same way as individual works with opus or thematic index numbers.

Example 12: M   Bach, Johann Sebastian, 1685-1750.
               24   [Suites, harpsichord, *BWV 812-817*]
               .B33
               S.812-817

D2: OTHER COLLECTIONS OF WORKS BY ONE COMPOSER

Collections of works by one composer have a second work number utilizing one letter and one digit to represent the editor or publisher. This technique is also used in classes that represent particular musical forms for collections of the works of one composer in that particular form.

Example 13: M   Obrecht, Jacob, d. 1505.
            3   [Works]
            .O27   Opera omnia ... edidit A. *Sm*ijers ...
            S6

            M   Haydn, Joseph, 1732-1809.
            23   [Sonatas, piano]
            .H39   Sonaten ... hrsg. yon C. A. *M*artienssen ...
            M3

Optionally, collections of works by one composer in a musical genre that is not represented by a particular class (e.g., nocturnes, impromptus, etc.) may be distinguished from more broadly based collections (e.g., Piano music. Selections) by addition of the digit "1" to the work number representing the composer. This is an artificial device that will allow two separate alphabetical sequences to distinguish the two types of collections when they must be classified together. In addition, this will prevent interfiling of works double-cuttered for editor with those double-cuttered for title. This is primarily a problem with piano music.

Example 14: M   Chopin, Frédéric, 1810-1849.
            22   [Piano music]
            .C56   Klavier ... hrsg. von Ignaz *Fr*iedman ...
            F7

            M   Chopin, Frédéric, 1810-1849.
            22   [Piano music. Selections]
            .C56   Forty piano compositions ... edited by
            H8   James *Hu*neker ...

            M   Chopin, Frédéric, 1810-1849.
            22   [*Im*promptus, piano]
            .C56*1*
            *I*4

            M   Chopin, Frédéric, 1810-1849.
            22   [*Pr*eludes, piano]
            .C56*1*
            P7

E: DRAMATIC VOCAL WORKS
E1: TRANSLATIONS

For dramatic vocal works (operas, oratorios, cantatas, etc.) for which it is desirable to distinguish various translations of the text, a second digit is added to the double-cutter to represent the language of the translation of the sung or spoken text. If the item has text in two or more languages, the digit should represent that language named first in the uniform title. These digits are derived from the translation table (Table 7).

Example 15: M   Bizet, Georges, 1838-1875.
               1503   [Carmen. Vocal score. *English* &
               .B59   French]
               C32

E2: MASSES

Because the uniform titles for masses frequently begin with some form of the word "mass," the part of the work number representing the title is based on a distinctive or keyword in the uniform title.

Example 16: M   Ockeghem, Johannes, ca. 1410-1497.
               2011   [Missa *Ca*put]
               .O34
               C3

F: EXCERPTS

For excerpts that have distinctive titles, a digit representing the title of the excerpt is added after the work number for the title of the complete work.

Example 17: M   La Montaine, John.
               2095   [Songs of the nativity. *N*ativity morn]
               .L35
               S66

   For numbered excerpts, the number is used following the distinguishing element or double-cutter for the complete work.

Example 18: M   Ysaye, Eugene, 1858-1931.
42   [Sonatas, violin, op. 27. *No. 3*]
.Y72
op. 27
no. 3

M   Cowell, Henry, 1897-1965.
233   Hymn and fuguing tune *no. 9* ...
.C69
H9
no. 9

G: EDITIONS AND ARRANGEMENTS
G1: ARRANGEMENTS

When it is necessary to resolve a conflict, arrangements can be distinguished by adding an extra digit (from Table 5) to the work number for the title or by adding an additional work number consisting of one letter and one digit (from Tables 1-4) following a distinguishing element to represent the arranger. If the work was arranged by its original composer, this element represents that composer's name.

Example 19: M   Debussy, Claude, 1862-1918.
223   [Printemps; arr.]
.D42   Printemps ... arr. par Jacques *D*urand ...
P73

M   Rejcha, Josef, 1746-1795.
1017   [Concertos, violoncello, orchestra, op.
.R44   2. No. 2; arr.]
op. 2   Konzert ... hrsg. und bearb. yon B.
no. 2   *Hu*mmel ...
H8

Optionally, distinguish all arrangements in this fashion.

G2: EDITIONS

Editions are distinguished by the addition of the date of publication as the final element of the call number. When the date of publication in the bibliographic description is incomplete or uncertain, dashes *are* represented by zeroes and the letter "z" is added (e.g., [19--] = 1900z; [197-] = 1970z; [1979?] = 1979z).[1]

Example 20: M Mendelssohn-Bartholdy, Felix, 1809-1847.
    2003 [Elias. Vocal score. English]
    .M46 Elijah ... *New ed.* ... *1903* ...
    E52
    1903

    M Verdi, Giuseppe, 1813-1901.
    1500 [Ballo in maschera]
    .V47 Un ballo in maschera ... *[18--]* ...
    B3
    1800z

G3: ISSUES

Optionally, if the size and use of a collection warrant such specificity, a combination of work numbers and dates may be used to distinguish issues of various editions. If this practice is adopted it is best to first add an extra digit (from Table 5) to the work number for title, or an additional work number consisting of one letter and one digit (from Tables 1-4) following a distinguishing element to represent the editor or publisher (in that order of preference). Later issues of each edition may then be distinguished by adding the date of issue as the final element.

Example 21: M Mozart, Wolfgang Amadeus, 1756-1791.
    1026 [Concertos, bassoon, orchestra, K. Anh.
    .M69 C14.03, B ♭ major]
    K.Anh. Konzert Nr. 2 ... hrsg. von Max
    C14.03 *Seiffert* ... *[1962]* ...
    S4
    1962

[Note: the original edition is dated 1934.]

Notes

1. More extensive discussion of LC's policy for editions is in "Shelflisting," p. 20. While the problems there addressed are not all common to musical editions, the reader may nevertheless find it useful.

Glossary

arrangement. "A musical work, or a portion thereof, rewritten for a medium of performance different from that for which the work was originally intended; a simplified version of a work for the same medium of performance."[1]

author number. A work number representing the author's name. *See also* **work number.**

bibliographic description. The completed catalog record for a specific library item.

book number. *See* **work number.**

call number. The complete alphanumeric symbol assigned to a specific library item for purposes of shelf location, retrieval, etc., consisting of any or all of the following: classification, work number(s), distinguishing element(s), date of publication.

class. *See* **classification.**

classification. Specific alphanumeric symbol assigned from a *Library of Congress Classification* schedule to represent the subject, form or intellectual content of a specific library item; the first element of a call number.

collection. An item comprised of more than one work. *See also* **separate.**

cuttering. The process of assigning a work number.

cutter number. A work number. *See also* **work number.**

distinctive title. The first element of a uniform title for a musical composition whose title does *not* consist of the name(s) of type(s) of composition (e.g., *Die Zauberflöte*, *Peer Gynt*, etc.); also a generic title that does not equate with the name of the class (e.g., *Suite* in a class for String quartets). *See also* **generic title; uniform title.**

distinguishing elements. Those parts of the uniform title (for a musical composition with a generic title) that are used to differentiate among compositions with similar titles.

double cutter. Two work numbers used together (e.g., .M69 P3); also, the second of two work numbers. *See also* **work number.**

dramatic vocal works. Operas, oratorios, cantatas, masses, etc.

edition. "All copies produced from essentially the same type image (whether by direct contact or by photographic or other methods) and issued by the same entity."[2] *See also* **issue.**

excerpt. A portion (or portions) of a musical composition published as an independent unit.

generic title. The first element of a uniform title for a musical composition whose title consists solely of the name(s) of type(s) of composition (e.g., concerto, nocturne, prelude and fugue, sonata, symphony, etc.). *See also* **distinctive title; uniform title.**

issue. "The whole number of copies of an edition put on sale at any time or times as a consciously planned unit."[3] *See also* **edition.**

item. The physical representation of a work; the entity forming the basis for a single bibliographic description. *See also* **work.**[4]

opus number. A number assigned to a musical composition, generally by the publisher or composer, to represent the order of composition; also, a distinguishing element in a uniform title or call number. *See also* **distinguishing elements; thematic index number.**

separate. An item consisting of a single work or part of a work. *See also* **collection; excerpt.**

serial number. Enumeration of a musical composition indicating the order of composition or publication; also, a distinguishing element in a uniform title or call number. *See also* **distinguishing elements.**

shelflist. A record of library items arranged in the order in which they stand on the shelves.

shelflisting. The process by which the classification number assigned to a specific library item is expanded into a call number unique to that item and then inserted into the shelving sequence represented by the shelflist.

thematic index. "A list of a composer's works, usually arranged in chronological order or by categories, with the theme [or musical incipit] given for each composition or for each section of large compositions."[5]

thematic index number. A unique number assigned by the compiler of a thematic index to each composition represented therein; also, a distinguishing element in a uniform title or call number. *See also* **distinguishing elements; opus number.**

title work number. A work number representing the title of the work. *See also* **work number.**

uniform title. That part of the bibliographic description for a musical work used to collocate bibliographic descriptions of a work that has appeared under varying titles proper, or of items containing several works or extracts from several works. A uniform title may be comprised of any or all of the following: title, medium of performance, opus/thematic index/serial number(s), key, date of composition, and language of translation of sung or spoken text.

work. A musical composition; the intellectual content of the item being catalogued and/or shelflisted. *See also* **item.**

work number. The alphanumeric symbol derived from Tables 1-5 that represents a name (composer, editor, arranger, publisher), title, language, instrument, text, etc. *See also* **author number; cutter number; double cutter; title work number.**

Notes

1. *Anglo-American Cataloguing Rules*, 2nd ed., 2002 revision (Chicago: American Library Association, 2002), p. D-1.

2. *AACR2*, p. D-3.

3. Fredson Bowers, *Principles of Bibliographical Description* (New York: Russell & Russell, 1949), p. 40.

4. See *The Nature of A Work* (Lanham, MD: Scarecrow Press, 2001); David H. Thomas and Richard P. Smiraglia, "Beyond the Score," *Notes: Quarterly Journal of the Music Library Association* 54 (1998), pp. 649-66; and Richard P. Smiraglia, "Musical Works and Information Retrieval," *Notes* 58 (2002), pp. 747-64.

5. *AACR2*, p. D-8. For a more detailed discussion see Barry S. Brook, *Thematic Catalogues in Music* (Hillsdale, N.Y. : Pendragon Press, 1972).

The Library of Congress Music Shelflist

[Excerpted from *Subject Cataloging Manual. Shelflisting*, G800, p. 1.]

The music shelflist was begun in the Music Division in 1904. At that time, a system of cuttering, different from that used in other classes, was devised for subclasses M, ML, and MT. As a part of the transfer of music cataloging from the Music Division to the Processing Department, the music shelflist was transferred in 1943 to the Subject Cataloging Division, where the main part of the shelflist was housed. There was an effort made to coordinate music shelflisting methods with those used in the main shelflist. The result was that new methods of shelflisting were created, adding to those inherited from the Music Division. Several methods of cuttering may be found in the same class, and it is sometimes difficult to determine which pattern to follow when a new entry is introduced. In 1957, when the then Music Section was established, the music shelflist was moved to the Descriptive Cataloging Division. The Music Section performed the descriptive and subject cataloging, as well as the shelflisting, of most music materials. After the cataloging reorganization of 1992, this arrangement continued, with the music teams of the Special Materials Cataloging Division replacing the former Music Section. Many revisions of shelflisting processes have been made in an effort to improve, simplify, and rationalize the work. Where the introduction of new procedures would have meant extensive changes to older entries, new entries were made to fit into the old system. For example, if some of a composer's works are provided with opus numbers, some with serial numbers, and music published and received by the Library of Congress, not all items cataloged receive full call numbers. These materials fall into the category known as uncuttered classes. Books about music are shelflisted following the provisions for shelflisting other materials at the Library of Congress.

Flowcharts

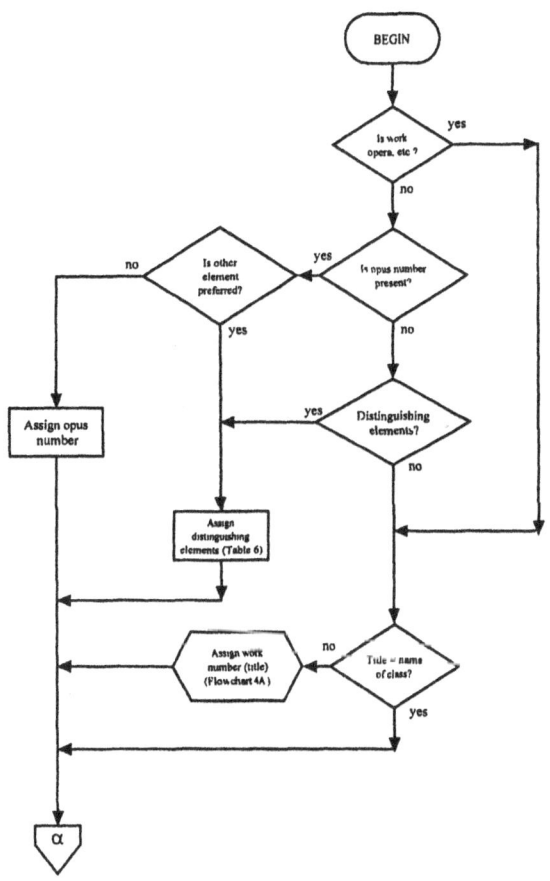

Flowchart 1

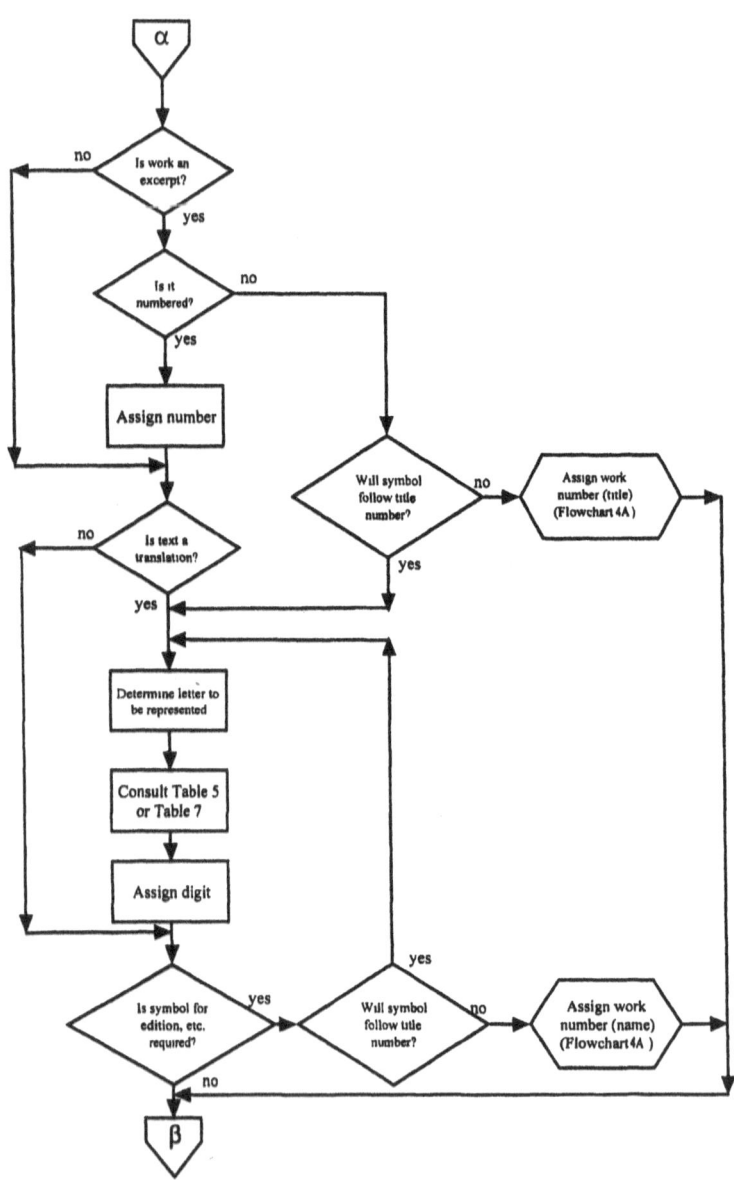

Flowchart 2

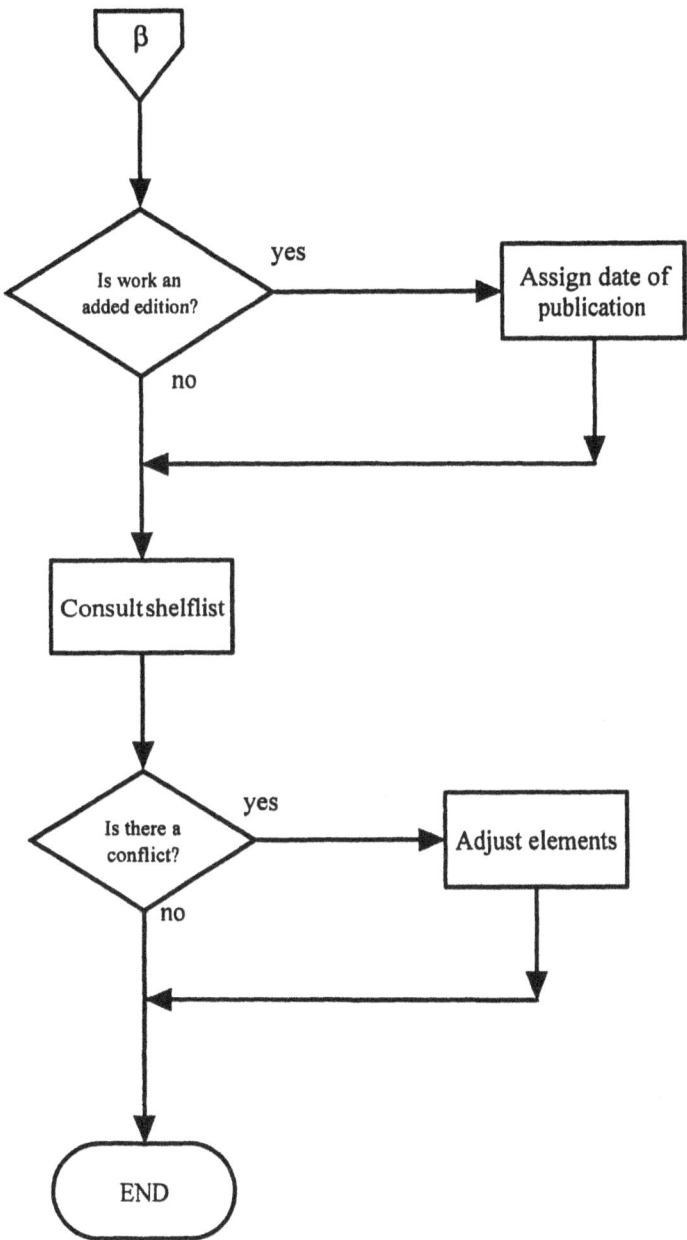

Flowchart 3

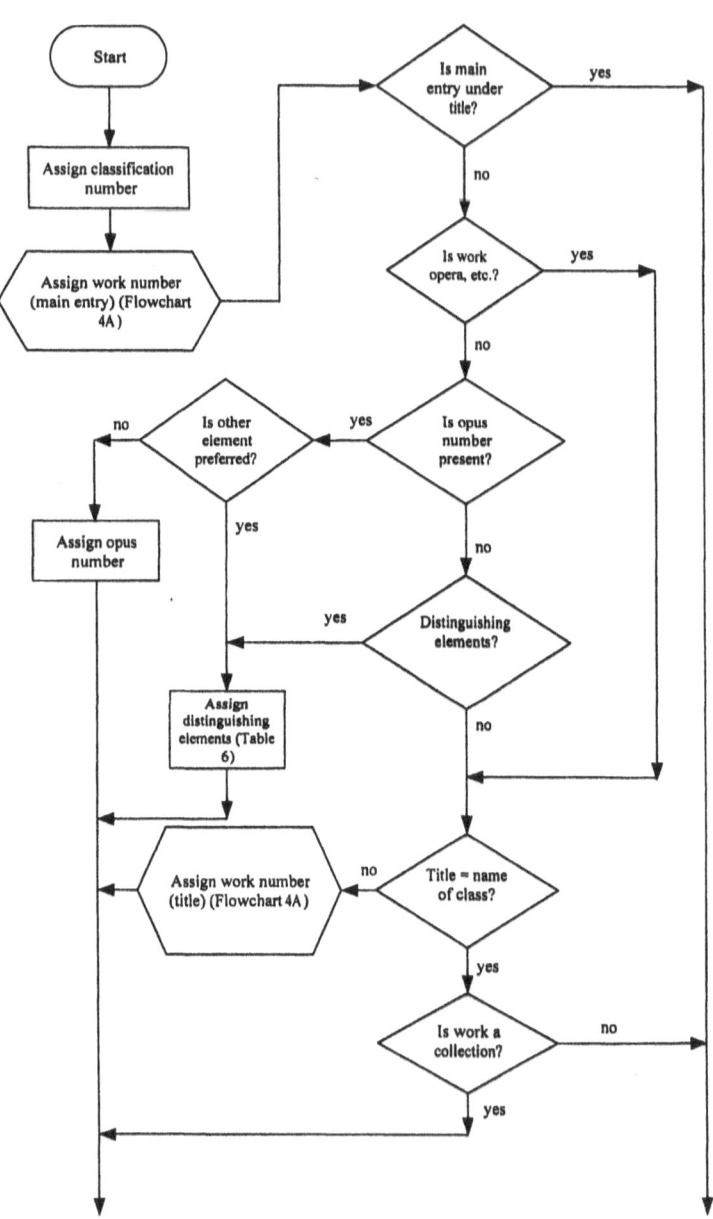

Flowchart 4

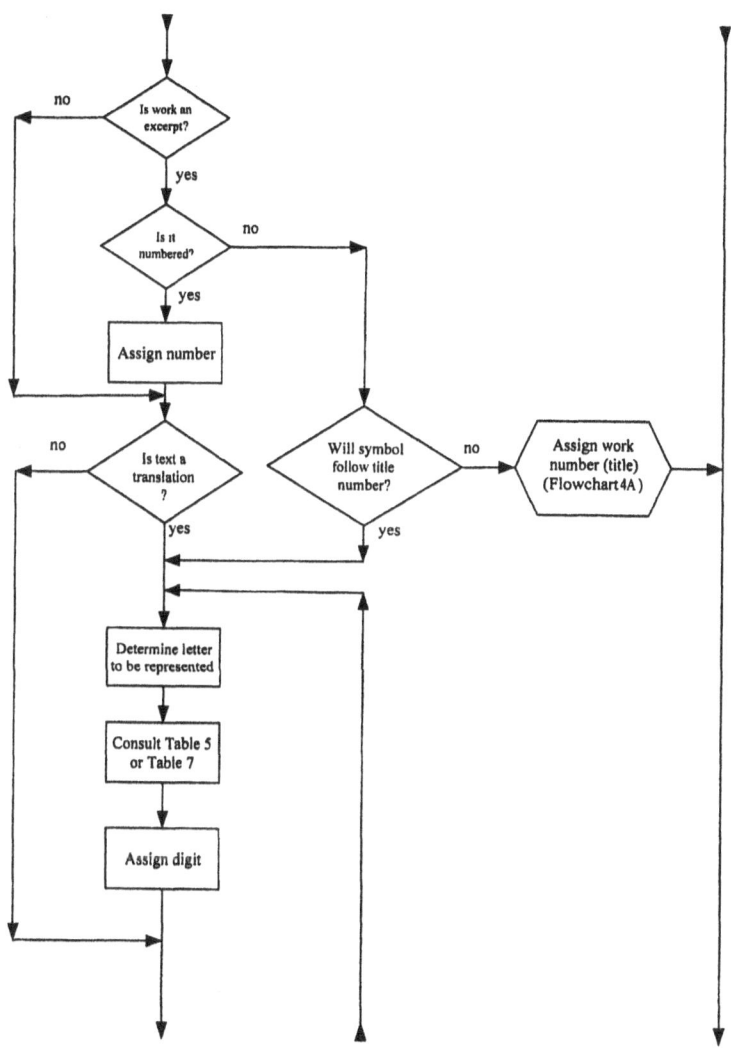

Flowchart 4 (continued from p. 32)

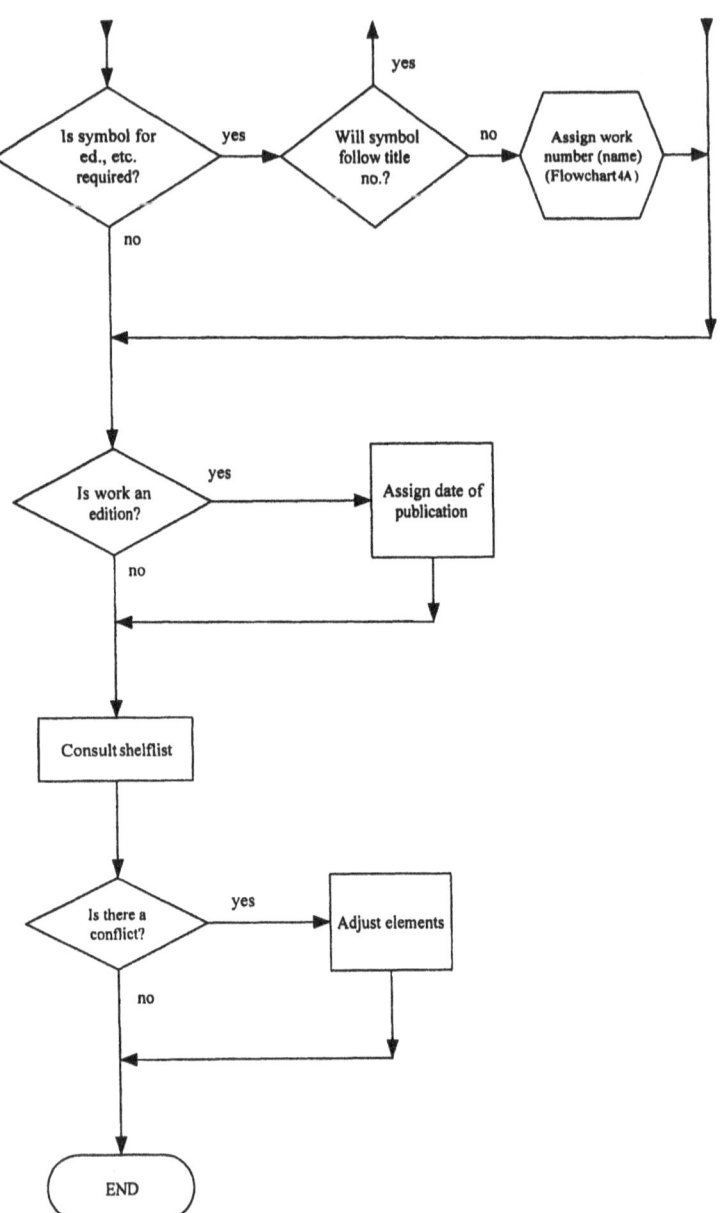

Flowchart 4 (continued from p. 33)

Flowcharts

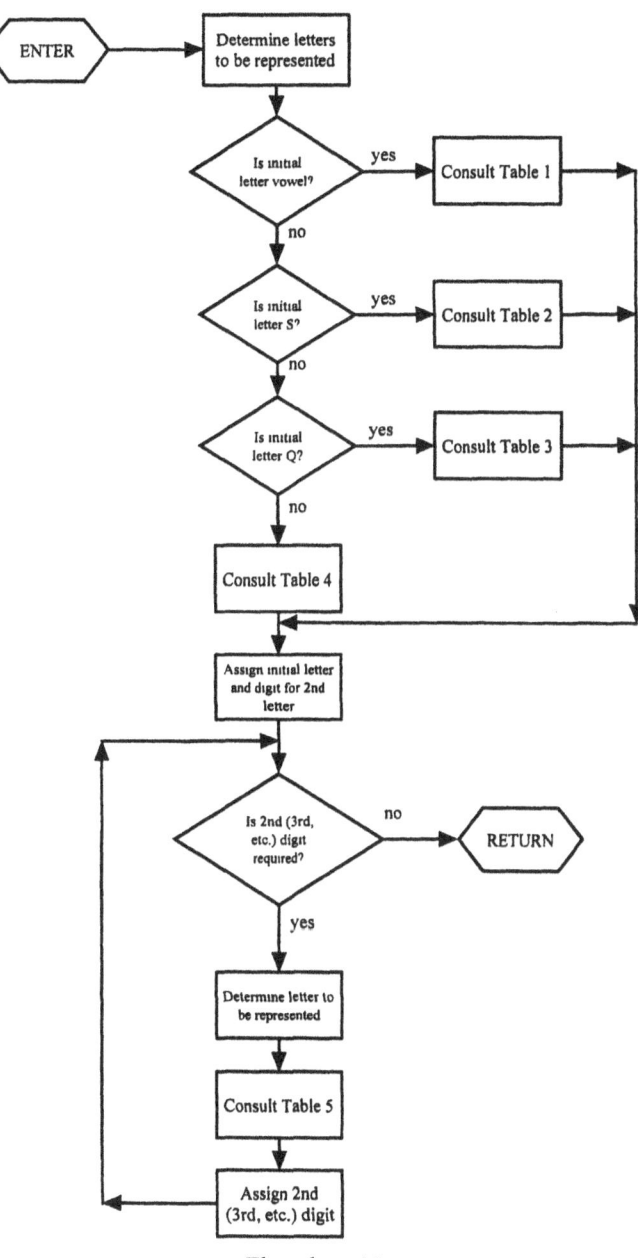

Flowchart 4A

About the Author

Richard P. Smiraglia, Ph.D., is professor at the Palmer School of Library and Information Science at Long Island University in Brookville, New York. He teaches courses in knowledge organization, broadly defined, and in research methods at the doctoral level. He has been with the Palmer School since 1992; prior to that he was assistant professor at Columbia University's School of Library Service, 1986-1992, and music catalog librarian at the University of Illinois at Urbana-Champaign, 1974-1986. He is the author of many books and monographs in the fields of knowledge organization, cataloging, and bibliography. He was editor of the journal *Library Resources & Technical Services* from 1990 to 1996 and the Music Library Association's "Technical Reports" series from 1988 to 1994. He is currently a member of the editorial board of *Cataloging & Classification Quarterly* and editor of the quarterly journal *Knowledge Organization*.

His 2001 monograph, *The Nature of "A Work": Implications for the Organization of Knowledge* was the first monograph-length treatment of the topic of works and their role in knowledge organization. In 2002 he edited *Works as Entities for Information Retrieval*, in which an international panel of authors focuses on domain-specific research about works and the problems inherent in their representation for information storage and retrieval. His most recent publications include *Bibliographic Control of Music, 1897-2000* (Scarecrow, 2006), "Authority Control of Works: Cataloging's Chimera?" (*Cataloging & Classification Quarterly* 38n3/4 (2004): 291-308), "The History of 'The Work' in the Modern Catalog" (*Cataloging & Classification Quarterly* 35n3/4 (2003): 553-67), "Works as Signs, Symbols, and Canons: The Epistemology of the Work" (*Knowledge Organization* 28 (2002): 192-202), and "Further Progress in Theory in Knowledge Organization" (*Canadian Journal of Information and Library Science* 26n2/3 (2002): 30-49).

www.ingramcontent.com/pod-product-compliance
Lightning Source LLC
Chambersburg PA
CBHW021801230426
43669CB00006B/162